FLYING WITH CLIPPED WINGS

Joyce Hope

Copyright © 2020 by **Joyce Hope**

All rights reserved. No part of this publication may be reproduced, distributed or transmitted in any form or by any means, including photocopying, recording, or other electronic or mechanical methods, without the prior written permission of the publisher, except in the case of brief quotations embodied in critical reviews and certain other noncommercial uses permitted by copyright law. For permission requests, write to the publisher, addressed "Attention: Permissions Coordinator," at the address below.

Joyce Hope/Rejoice Essential Publishing

PO BOX 512

Effingham, SC 29541

www.republishing.org

Unless otherwise indicated, scripture is taken from the King James Version.'

All Scripture quotations are taken from THE MESSAGE, copyright © 1993, 2002, 2018 by Eugene H. Peterson. Used by permission of NavPress, represented by Tyndale House Publishers. All rights reserved.

Flying With Clipped Wings/ Joyce Hope

ISBN-13: 978-1-952312-56-4
Library of Congress Control Number: 2021902294

FLYING WITH CLIPPED WINGS is a powerful book by Pastor Joyce Hope. Throughout her life, she faced rejection and was hindered by those who couldn't see her potential. When she was going through the motions in life, God spoke to her, "Flying with Clipped Wings." When she heard those words, a light bulb went off in her mind and she did her research. Inside this book, she will share revelatory information with you. We can all relate to Joyce's story because we have gone through trials and experienced setbacks and rejection. However, Joyce didn't quit and now we see her walking in her God-given purpose today. Let this book, "Flying with Clipped Wings," encourage you on your journey.

Kimberly Moses
Publisher and Author of Rejoice Essential Publishing

Dedication

*T*HIS BOOK IS DEDICATED to my mother, Annie E. Hope, whose strength I have inherited.

Ma, I miss you so much. You are always in my heart.

To my children, Shekinah and Philip, thank you so much for the many years of patiently riding with me through my deliverance process.

To my twin sister Doris, you are the wind beneath my wings. Thank you for helping me get my voice back.

To my shepherd Mother Hattie Green, you inspired me throughout the past 30 years to be who God called me to be

FLYING WITH CLIPPED WINGS

COLOR ME HUMAN

BY INDIGO SOUL

Color me human.
Color me Human.

For I am a perfectly painted
blemish created
in an imperfect image.

I have been shaped by mistakes.
Just hold a mirror up to my errors, and you can see reflections of life lessons upon
my face.
I am a victim of chance.

A poster child for trials.
I learned to walk by falling.
I stumbled over faults
until I learned to stack them
in piles.

COLOR ME HUMAN

My smile is bent.
My heart has a dent.
My beauty is a flaw that
"acceptance" reinvents.

I am a blessing known as flesh
and bone, I bleed, I breathe, and these scars
I own, show that with failure comes wings,
proven that I have grown.

I was born in sin, till born again, then
bruised by "He who cast the first stone."
My life is a vision imprisoned within decisions,
I've fallen and I have risen, and
I've died inside, murdered by pride but resuscitated by wisdom.

Judge me. Shrug me.
Hate Me. Love Me.
Push Me. Shove Me.
Accept Me. Reject Me.

Whether Beautiful or Ugly
Cover me until all truth is blooming.
Whether in darkness or in light, You must
Color Me Human!

~ S Hope

Contents

INTRODUCTION..1

CHAPTER 1:   My Beginning..6

CHAPTER 2:   What Is Normal..9

CHAPTER 3:   Why New York City?...............................12

CHAPTER 4:   The Red Jacket...16

CHAPTER 5:   Leaking Faucets.......................................21

CHAPTER 6:   Detours and Distractions......................26

CHAPTER 7:   Out of the Pan Into the Fire................33

CHAPTER 8:   Stuck..36

CHAPTER 9:   My Wilderness Experience...................38

CHAPTER 10:   The End of An Era/The End
               of An Error..43

CHAPTER 11:   Repeat Defender.....................................45

CHAPTER 12:   The Road to Recovery..........................49

CHAPTER 13:   Receipts..53

| CHAPTER 14: | Clipped Wings Can Still Soar.................55 |
| CHAPTER 15 | My Truths-My Realities-My Story..63 |

ABOUT THE AUTHOR..66

Introduction

TODAY TRANSPARENCY IS A must. The world is looking for real people who have endured real-life situations.

I've got a story that didn't start with me, but the mercy of God. — Pastor Steven Furtick.

For all of you who walk the straight and narrow line, this book may not be for you. Inside this book, you will read about the good, bad, and ugly truths and reality experienced in a woman's life. Today, she admits that she has made hundreds of mistakes, bad decisions, and horrible choices, most of them after being saved. Sometimes people will look at a person's present state but have no idea of the journey it took to get there. I'm so glad that God did not allow my past mistakes to dictate my future. The saying, "You see my glory, but you don't know my story," is relevant to this book.

Never be ashamed of a scar. It simply means you were stronger than whatever tried to hurt you— Author Unknown.

As you begin to read the pages of Flying With Clipped Wings, you will walk through the life of a woman who today is over 50 years old but has been on a rollercoaster ride throughout most of her life. She unveils her truths because she decided that she will no longer allow her past mistakes to define her God-given purpose. That woman is me. I admit that it was all a part of the Master's plan. There are people who have been in my life for over 30 years who did not know the untold details of my story. But today I declare I will no longer walk in bondage and condemnation, ashamed of my life. It had to happen and now let the healing process begin!

This book is in no way, shape, or form written to defame anyone's character. I am simply obeying God. The Word of God states in Revelation 12:11, "And they overcame him by the blood of the Lamb, and by the word of their testimony." This book is written to bring hope and encouragement to anyone who may have found themselves in situations that are beyond their control that they will look to Jesus for their salvation and deliverance.

Therefore, I pray in the name of Jesus that God will touch every person who reads this book. Whatever they need, I pray that God will show Himself strong and mighty in their lives. In Jesus' name, I pray that God will save, heal, deliver, and set them free from the bondages and chains that bind. I speak the blessings of God upon your life in Jesus' name, Amen.

Introduction

As I was preparing to minister the Word of God at the birthday appreciation service for my Shepherd Mother (Mother Hattie Green), the Holy Spirit spoke the words, "Flying with Clipped Wings" to me. I rehearsed it over and over in my mind and although it was a strange word, it was definitely on point. I had never heard of clipped wings. So I researched it and found out there was really something known as clipped wings. As I began to read its definition, I found that this was confirmation that I definitely had heard from the Holy Spirit. I've heard of broken wings before, but never clipped wings. Broken wings are most likely to occur accidentally, but clipped wings are intentional. When a bird's wings are clipped, it is done on purpose by its owner so that the bird cannot fly at its full potential. There are times when we find ourselves in relationships and come in agreement with people who do not want to see us fly at our maximum performance ability. Because of their own insecurities about who they are, people will try to devalue you and your possibility of using your wings. This behavior can come from your relatives, friends or even your co-workers on your job. Clipped Wings.

According to an article written on January 27, 2011, by Dr. Becker, "This is a never-ending controversy. It is very important to understand both sides of the issue. Birds are creatures of the air. Birds fly for necessity and for pleasure. Flying is a natural instinct for a bird. Last but not least, there are several reasons for flight:

1. to find food,
2. to find other birds including mating
3. to find breeding and nesting sites
4. to escape danger and predation and
5. to find parties, opportunities to socialize.

I've served at the ministry for over 30 years; therefore, I was well acquainted with my Shepherd Mother. She has endured some fiery trials throughout the years. I sat silently, watching, and praying for her. I knew the topic was the best description of her journey, but I was hesitant. After several days, I surrendered and said, "Yes, Lord. I'll say what you want me to say. Needless, to say, To God Be the Glory for the deliverance that took place in that church on that night. The birthday appreciation service turned into a revival after the altar call. Shepherd Mother was encouraged and overjoyed. She said she received the Word of God and it was exactly what she needed. To God be the Glory.

Several days later, the Holy Spirit continued to minister to me concerning the clipped wings. As I listened to Him, tears began to roll down my face because at that moment, I realized that the Word of God was for me first. I've been flying (living) with clipped wings all my life. I've never had a full set of wings. First of all, my mother thought she was having one baby and ended up with two. I was not born with a silver spoon in my mouth. I was a sickly child, suffering with asthma and anemia most of my childhood. I came from Accomack County, Virginia. I was raised on welfare and food stamps. I came from a single parent home, eating leftovers for days until it was all gone. We

Introduction

wore no-name brand sneakers and clothing, but we were clean and well-groomed. But God was with me...Flying with Clipped Wings.

CHAPTER 1:

My Beginning

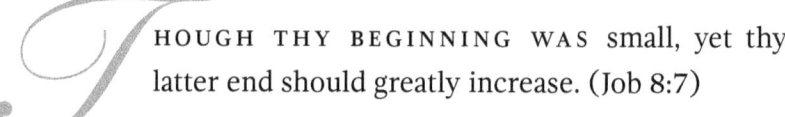

THOUGH THY BEGINNING WAS small, yet thy latter end should greatly increase. (Job 8:7)

I am the youngest of an unexpected set of twins born in a house on a Saturday night in Accomack, Virginia, to a single mother (Clipped Wings). My mother did not know she was carrying twin girls until after the birth of my twin sister. The midwife said, "Oh, it's another one in there!" That was me!

"Thou hast covered me in my mother's womb" (Psalm 139:13b).

I also have another sister, who is nine years older than us. We had a brother named James, who died at the age of 6 years old from polio. Polio is an infectious disease most commonly affecting children under the age of 5. It can affect a person's spinal cord causing paralysis. There is no cure but preventable with a vaccine. After his death, my mother moved her three daughters to New York in search of a better life. But was it really a better life? Only God knows. We left a familiar place of poverty, hurt, pain, and loss. Jobs were hard to find in Accomack,

My Beginning

Virginia, at that time. I'm positive that my aunts encouraged my mother to take that leap of faith to move to New York City. Nevertheless, I know it was all God orchestrated.

Even as young as five years old, I knew that God was real. I remember sitting at the dinner table, halfway on the chair to leave room for God to sit next to me. Silly me, so young and innocent. God is a Spirit and He is everywhere (John 4:24). We were raised in the Bedford-Stuyvesant section of Brooklyn, New York. My earliest memory of being in New York is my twin sister and I playing outside the house on Hancock Street and Tompkins Avenue. It was our first apartment when we moved from Virginia in the late 1960s.

My mother worked very hard to provide for her three daughters. I remember leaving home early in the mornings so that my mother could drop us off at the babysitter, Miss Hall's house before she headed off to work. My next childhood memory is of us living on the top floor apartment at 511 Halsey Street next door to my Aunt Betty. She had two sons, Daryl and Dwayne, and they were more like our little brothers than cousins. It was at this residence that I recall most of my childhood memories. We were always outside with our cousins and the neighborhood kids running around playing games such as jacks, hide-and-go-seek, hopscotch, tag, pick up sticks, dodgeball, jump rope, skelly, etc., just enjoying life.

When we couldn't go outside, we played in the hallway with our cousins. Although we shared many childhood memories, this is where my life was changed forever. During a recent teaching on the subject of The Spirit of Death and the Orphan (Fatherlessness) from the Scripture of Isaiah 10:2 and John 10:10, Apostle John Eckhardt stated, "The enemy wants to rob the fatherless of their destiny, future, vision, purpose, and strength to take advantage of them."

CHAPTER 2

What Is Normal?

BISHOP T.D. JAKES SAID, "Your normal and my normal have two different meanings." When you are a child, you do not know what is supposed to be normal. What you see every day is what's normal for you. But that doesn't mean it's normal. Who can explain normal? If you grew up in a single-parent household like I did, you might have experienced a mother who worked hard to make ends meet. That was my normal. If you grew up in a two-parent home where they fussed, argued, and fought all the time, that is what you may consider being normal. Maybe you grew up with two parents who loved each other and loved and served God. For you, that may be considered a normal life. It's not until you see and hear something different that you realize this is not normal. But what is normal? Who can explain normal?

Every family has some form of dysfunction in it. So who gets to define what's normal? Let me give you an example from my life. I knew who my father was and I had always wished that my daddy lived with us, so that he could provide and protect us. I think that's every little girl's dream. But unfortunately, we didn't have that privilege. It wasn't until I talked to my older brother and my younger sisters, who lived in the same household with him, that I realized we were covered by God. (Father God knows what's best). The picture they painted was that we were better off without him in our home. My father was an alcoholic who fought with their mom all the time. That was the norm for them. What seems to be normal for one person may be a dysfunction for another person.

I knew we didn't have a lot of money, but my mother made sure we had a place to stay, food to eat and clothes to wear, all without my father's financial support. I can recall the book of food stamps. We had to rip them out one by one in the store to give to the clerk for food purchases. I also remember the block of government cheese and the can of peanut butter. My mother made the best macaroni and cheese I've ever tasted with that government cheese.

In my childlike mind, I wanted what other children had, but I knew I couldn't have it. My mother's priority was to make sure the bills were paid. When she did have a little extra money, we would walk to Broadway and she would buy us only the things that we needed. We did not always get what we wanted. We dared not complain because she was making the best out of what we had. If you even seemed ungrateful, that would bring on a long fussing session that we would soon regret. When she finally finished, we were relieved. I learned to live with less and appreciate whatever I had. It wasn't easy because children can be crude. They made jokes that hurt, not realizing that we were all in the same boat. Life was hard for me as a kid. But God brought us through it.

What Is Normal?

As I've matured over the years, I've learned more about myself and the things that make me happy. Growing up poor helped me to stay humble. I'm not materialistic at all, but now I ask myself why should I live beneath my privileges when God, my Father has everything and everything belongs to Him? How do you define normal?

Nothing changes if nothing changes. – Author Unknown

CHAPTER 3

Why New York City?

*G*OD LED THEM NOT through the way of the land of the Philistines although it was near. — (Exodus 13:17)

The plan of God will take you out of your comfort zone. I've traveled down some roads in my life that I have no idea of how I got there or where I was going. My life became a revolving door. As children, we imagined how our life would turn out. We playfully planned who we would marry, what kind of job we would have, where we would live, and how many children we would have and so on. We fantasize all the time with all that our little minds could imagine. For some of us, life served us a different hand.

As far as I know, both of my parents and my grandparents were from Accomack, Virginia. It would have been the most obvious place for us to be raised, but God had a different plan. Just like Moses, being sent down a river and saved from the plot of Pharaoh, God spared his life and instead of being put

Why New York City?

to death like the other boys, God allowed Moses to live in the King's palace. God used him to perform some mighty works for Him. How about Jesus, saved from the plot of King Herod. Only God knows what He saved us from in Accomack, Virginia. To God be the Glory!

My memories of living in New York City brings tears of joy, and tears of sadness. I've experienced so many things from the age of 4 to 40 years old that shaped me into the woman I am today. Who would imagine that something good would come out of Accomack County, Virginia on the Eastern Shore? God did. He knew I would eventually accept who I am in Him and rise above the low expectations of my family and friends. They thought that because of who my daddy was (an alcoholic) and who my mother was (a single parent) and where I was born or even because of the color of my skin that I would turn out to be nothing but a product of my environment.

Romans 8:31 says, "What shall we then say to these things, if God be for us, who can be against us?"

New York has been my grooming place, my boot camp. The lessons I've learned while living in New York have prepared me to know that I can make it anywhere I go in life. There is a song titled, "New York New York." There is a line in that song that says, "If I can make it there, I'll make it anywhere." I've met some amazing people. Most importantly, I've crossed paths with real men and women of God who took time to teach me about God and His Word guiding me into my destiny. I've always believed in God and I knew that God was with me.

My first spiritual encounter with God as I remember it was when I was about 12 years old. God sent the Moore family to relocate into our neighborhood. They were a large blended family of 9 kids. The oldest daughter was our age and we quickly became friends with them. They invited us to go to church with them. It was a Pentecostal Holiness Church. At first, it was strange to us because we were used to the quiet Baptist church down the street. This church was lively. We stayed in church all day on Sunday, which included Sunday school, and attended three services every week: prayer on Tuesdays, bible study on Wednesday, and Friday night service. They kept us so busy so that we had no choice but to stay focused on God. At first, my mother was concerned about us going so much and sometimes getting home late at night, but after a while she just let us continue to go. Today I am so glad she did because this is where I got my foundation in God.

Soon after, I learned that this church was not boring. At a revival in 1978, I felt the undeniable, tangible presence of the Holy Spirit for the very first time. The Holy Spirit drew me in. At the age of 14 years old, I accepted Jesus Christ as my personal Savior. Thank God, I know He saved me from my sins, yet I still experienced some other things. I did not totally understand what I was getting into, but I knew I wanted whatever it was. The pastors and ministers took time to teach us how to live a holy saved life. We learned the importance of having a prayer life. Sometimes on Saturdays, we went to the hospitals and nursing homes to visit and pray with the patients.

Why New York City?

They kept us busy, but that was good training for me. We learned how to carry ourselves as saved young ladies in school. This was the beginning of my spiritual Christian journey. I do not regret my path, although I did not understand it all the time. It seemed hard at times, with so many rules of do's and don'ts, but today I am so grateful to God. This was my foundation. Now that I look back over my beginning, I realize there was a lot of legalism being taught, something that was only passed down from the previous generations. For example, rules about wearing pants and giving us the Scripture from Deuteronomy 22:5, "Women wearing that which pertaineth to a man."

They interpreted that as being pants were men's garments and women should not wear them. They could not answer the question when presented with "Why do they make women's pants?" I didn't attend my high school prom because they made us feel that it was a sin. Why New York? It was the place where God sent me to be trained for my spiritual journey. I cannot express how appreciative I am that God ordered my steps. I was born in Accomack, Virginia, but I was raised in Brooklyn, New York. God protected us from the negative influence of that environment. God covered me.

CHAPTER 4

The Red Jacket

UNFORTUNATELY, I DO HAVE some bad memories of New York. Let me share just a few with you. At around the age of 10, I got hit by a car while crossing the street. I had the red light to cross the street, but the driver allowed the car to continue to roll slowly without paying attention. As I ran across the street, the car hit me, knocking me down. I didn't get hurt, but I was taken to the hospital to be checked out. To show his sincere apology, the owner of the car bought me a bicycle. That bicycle caused my twin sister and me to have a lot of fights. I was supposed to share my bicycle with her until my mother could afford to purchase one for her. That never happened. I was so selfish. I did not want her to ride my bike, and when she did, it was only for a few minutes. That made her mad at me.

Another unforgettable memory is being unexpectedly picked up and thrown into a swimming pool. It was a horrifying experience because I did not know how to swim. This happened on a Saturday bus outing to a water park. Someone picked me up from behind and threw me in the pool. I remember going to the bottom and floating back up to the top gasping for air and someone pulled me out of the water. As a result, I had an asthma attack and I had to be rushed to the hospital later that night.

When I got saved, God healed me from asthma. At the age of 18, right after graduation from high school, I received sexual advancements and invitations from one of the married pastors in the church. A month after my high school graduation, he bought me a gift to persuade me to be his girlfriend, but that didn't work. But the most traumatic and most memorable experience of all was at the age of around seven years old. I was sexually violated by an older cousin. I just found out recently that my twin sister had a similar experience from the same cousin. It happened at my Aunt Betty's house. Whenever the adults wanted to talk about private stuff, they always sent the kids next door to play. On this particular day, an older cousin was visiting and he followed us across the hall to my aunt's apartment. I do not recall all of the details of what happened to me that day because I have suppressed it. I still have a mental memory of the pain. For me, instead of sex being pleasurable as God ordained in marriage, it has been traumatic. He touched me inappropriately. It was determined, after a brief counseling session, that he tried to penetrate me. I was only seven years old, and I was exposed to a lustful and perverted spirit. This incident has caused my childhood to be turned into years of unwanted sexual desires. As I got older, the desires came, but the fear of the pain of penetration did not allow me to be promiscuous.

Yes, I got saved at the age of 14 years old, but I was in need of deliverance from those unclean spirits. The saints never discerned my need for deliverance. I didn't bother to tell them. Even to this day, some act as though they haven't sinned. The truth of the matter is they think no one knows about their hidden sins. Some are quick to talk and gossip about a person, but they failed to understand that it is a spiritual battle for this person. It was for me. We need to stop judging the things that we do not understand, and let us pray one for another.

James 5:16 states, "Confess your faults one to another, and pray one for another, that ye may be healed. The effectual fervent prayer of a righteous man availeth much. "

These are my truths, my reality and my story and in the words of Bishop George Bloomer, "can't nobody tell my story better than me!" This chapter is dedicated to my God-sister, the late Pastor Tammy Moore. Tammy will always be remembered as a bubbly, loving, compassionate person who loved to sing. I have dedicated this chapter to Tammy because our last telephone conversation was about my red jacket.

In 2016 our former church was preparing for a reunion. Everyone was excited about coming together. I wholeheartedly planned to be there, but financially I was struggling. I was newly divorced and the added expenses of a weekend away were out of my budget. A week before the set date, Tammy called me and asked whether I was coming to the reunion. When I expressed my doubts, she encouraged me to try hard to be there. She mentioned the red jacket I had on in my Facebook picture.

The Red Jacket

Tammy wanted to be sure that this was not a fake page. After I told her that it was me, we laughed about it. I somehow managed to make it to the last day of the reunion. While others ignored me because I missed the other two days, Tammy made sure that she greeted me as we briefly chatted before she left to go home. The following month, Tammy passed away with a brain aneurysm. Unbeknownst to all of us, this would be the last time we would see Tammy alive.

Anyone who really knows me knows that I've always had a red jacket. I became attached to my red jacket at around the age of 8 years old. I wore this red jacket every single day everywhere I went, all summer long. Even when it was over 100 degrees outside, I wore my red jacket. My sisters and friends would constantly tease me. I wore this red jacket to the park, to the store, everywhere I went I had on this red jacket. The red jacket became my best friend. For many years, I did not understand what the red jacket represented. A couple of years ago, as I was riding with my niece talking about some things that I've been through that I never shared with anyone in our family, and it hit me. I had an "ah ha" moment. God revealed the significance of that red jacket. The red jacket was my security blanket. The red jacket protected me. It was used to cover my body and hide the guilt, shame, condemnation and embarrassment I was experiencing. I had been violated and I felt like everyone could see it on me.

The reality of the pain I held in for so many years was not revealed. I didn't trust my secret with anyone. I never talked about it until two years ago. A close friend started asking questions. We talked for hours until I was able to let down my wall. I went back into my childhood and I confessed what happened to me. It was then confirmed that my cousin tried to penetrate/rape me at seven years old. I felt that no one would understand. Condemnation gripped my life. I felt ashamed, alone, violated, and unprotected for many years. The red jacket became my best friend. I wore this red jacket and I wore clothes that were big on me because I did not want any attention drawn to my body. One night, I forgot my red jacket in someone's car and it was never returned or replaced. My false sense of protection was gone. Recently when I looked through my closet, I noticed that I have two red jackets. I really don't wear the color red a lot. Red is a vibrant, cheerful, happy color. For so many years, I avoided wearing the color red because of the attention I received.

CHAPTER 5

Leaking Faucets

Have you heard the saying, "Hurt people hurt people?" I am a witness that it is absolutely the truth. This is my truth, reality, and story. I was deeply hurt as a child and for many years, I carried the hurt. Now that I have openly admitted that I was sexually violated at a very young age, I feel so much lighter. This incident stole my self-worth. I walked in low self-esteem, shame, guilt, embarrassment, condemnation, lust, perversion, and unwanted sexual desires. Because of this, my life was altered; my wings were clipped. My thought pattern was interrupted. My focus was blurred. Centered on things that a little girl should not think about until she is much older. I was prematurely exposed to an adult world.

The sanctified saints did not discern that there was something wrong. There was one exception, a lady named Prophetess Tina. She was a powerful, anointed woman of God. She made a statement one day that let me know God revealed to her what I was struggling with. But she never mentioned it again, she didn't address me about it, nor did she pray for my deliverance. God had given her a word of knowledge, but she may have doubted it or just refused to obey God. This is the reason why being Spirit-led and being obedient to the Holy Spirit is very important. Someone is waiting for your obedience in order to get their breakthrough. I could have received the deliverance I needed.

I could not tell the saints what I was feeling, so I kept it to myself. Keeping it to myself did not help me. It hurt me. This caused me many years of walking around in bondage. The devil enjoyed it too because as long as I was quiet and bound, he didn't have to worry about me walking in the liberty that Jesus Christ provided by dying in my place to set me free. Not only was I hurting, but I hurt others who were very dear to my heart. I said things and did things that were hurtful because I was hurting. It caused me more damage than good because I caused damage to the lives of those around me. Hurt people really do hurt people.

Some things I didn't remember what I had done, but when they were brought to my attention, I was heartbroken. I apologized immediately. I prayed that they would forgive me and that God would heal them from the hurt I caused them. Not to make any excuses, but I grew up without experiencing a lot of affection. I did not receive any hugs, compliments, words of encouragement and affirmations. I do not recall hearing the words "I love you," or "I'm proud of you." I felt rejected my entire childhood. I felt like I was a mistake. Thoughts of suicide crossed my mind several times. "They will not miss you," the devil whispered in my ear. I can count on one hand the number of times I heard my mother say she loved me. She had experienced some traumatic situations while growing up. It actually was generational, passed down from my mother to me and now from me to my daughter.

There has only been one occasion when I can recall hearing my mother publicly say that she was proud of me. It was November 27, 1988, at an appreciation service given in my honor by the youth department of New Life Pentecostal Holiness Church. I loved my mother so dearly, but I've always felt like I was a burden to her. So here I am dealing with the spirit of rejection as well. Like I mentioned earlier, she worked very hard to support her children. That was her way of showing us that she loved us. Sometimes we would be fussed at and a lot of negative words were spoken out of her bitterness and anger towards my "no-good daddy." It was very toxic but I knew she didn't really mean it. Words carry damage beyond repair. Once they leave your lips, you cannot get them back. I recall one time she said, "I despise you." At the time, I did not know what despise meant, but the tone of her voice repeatedly rang in my head over the years. When I read that Jesus was despised and rejected in Isaiah 53:3, I was encouraged to know that He knows my pain of rejection.

I unwillingly too experienced the frustrations of being a single parent. There are some things that are unknowingly passed on to the next generation. We call them generational curses. It is not until you acknowledge it and renounce it, that the curse can be broken. If not, it will carry on into the next generation and so on and so on. Regrettably, that is what has happened with me. I did the same to my children, repeating the same toxic behavior, speaking words of negativity instead of words of affirmation and encouragement. I loved my mother dearly, but some of the things I did was because it was done to me. I became a leaky faucet because of my past abuse and neglect.

Today I regret not being a more positive role model to my children. But I could not give them what I did not have myself. I was a damaged soul. My unresolved issues with my abuse and my abuser caused me a lot of pain. Even though it was not my fault, I allowed my hurt to affect all areas of my life. Do you know that if a leaking faucet is constantly dripping, it will cause damage to everything and everyone around it? I was hurting and bitter and angry. I was very negative and unwilling to see any good in anything. I lived in denial of my need for healing. I was bleeding on people who did not hurt me, but they loved me.

One day my daughter called me a Grinch. My feelings were hurt, but I looked it up in the Merriam Webster dictionary. It is defined as a killjoy, a party pooper, an unpleasant person who spoils other people's fun. I didn't even realize that I was doing that. Years ago, one of my brothers in Christ said I was cantankerous. I ignored him. Years later, the Holy Spirit brought it back to my attention and I began to research its meaning. Collins English Dictionary describes a cantankerous person as someone who is always finding things to argue or complain about. Yes, that was me too. Cantankerous, that's exactly the word I would use to describe my life at that time. I had to admit it was true and face my reality. The problem was me, not everyone else.

What happened to me was not my fault, but now it became my responsibility to get the healing that I needed. Once I accepted my truth, I repented, asked for forgiveness, and then I began to work on me. I stopped focusing on my past and I began to rehearse the Word of God over my life. That's how I began my process of deliverance. It was not an overnight fix. It was a process that took several years. As time moved on, I started loving myself more and more. I've learned that I have to renounce those negative words spoken over my life. Ever since I started making daily confessions and commanding my day, I've felt so much freedom.

CHAPTER 6

Detours and Distractions

*P*ART OF REACHING YOUR destiny is in understanding your detours. — Dr. Tony Evans, Senior Pastor of Oak Cliff Bible Fellowship in Dallas, TX.

A detour is defined as an alternate route. Have you ever set your GPS to a certain address and didn't follow the directions it was giving you? All of a sudden, the voice activated system starts a new search for an alternate route. In order to get where you want to go, the GPS now has to reprogram itself. I remember one time the GPS told me that I was at my destination, but I still could not find the building. Just like the GPS, I had to "reset" my life. I finally recognized that the decisions I chose were not working for me.

God has a divine plan and purpose for your life. God has the roadmap to get you there. When we choose to take matters into our own hands, we without saying it tell God I got this. Well, God being the gentleman that He is, will step aside and wait patiently for you to come back to Him for help. When you do, He will then with open arms welcome you back.

I must confess that throughout my life, I've made mistakes over and over and over again. There were times that I thought I knew what was best for me. I found out I was wrong. To be totally honest, I kept doing my own thing, hoping things would change. This was the devil's way of keeping me distracted. As long as I stayed distracted, I could not focus on fulfilling the will of God for my life. For many years I experienced distraction after distraction. It got so bad that I felt like I was on a merry-go-round waiting for it to stop. The revolving door would not stop. It just kept going around and around and around. There are times that I did not recognize the distraction until after it had distracted me.

Distractions come in many different forms. For example, (and this is my truth) for many years, I was distracted from building my spiritual walk with God through TV. Yes, TV is a distraction. The many hours that I spent watching show after show for hours, I could have been reading and studying the Word of God. Also, people can be a distraction to your spiritual walk.

One major distraction came in my early 20's. At the age of 21, I was reunited with my high school crush. He was a minister and one of the very popular students in our class. He was known as "Rev." But unbeknownst to me, he lived a different lifestyle outside of church. I found all this out after we were married. I was naïve and didn't see the warning signs, which included inconsistency. In high school, we became good friends while working together after school at the library. But nothing blossomed from it. After graduation, we lost contact with one another.

After three years, while traveling to an afternoon service, he passed my church. I was standing outside in my usher uniform talking to one of the sisters at church. On that afternoon, we talked for a little while because he was on his way to an afternoon service so we exchanged telephone numbers. From that day forward, we started talking and then courting and soon began making plans to marry. A year and a half later, we got married. But a month after our big lavish wedding, he announced that he didn't want to be married and moved back home to his mother's house. I was devastated and terribly embarrassed. I became depressed. I lost a lot of weight, my hair fell out and I quit my good state job.

After a couple of years, I moved back home with my mom and worked temporary jobs to help with the bills. I was in a place where no one could help me but God. Instead of turning to God, I chose another man (distraction). Somebody say, "Big Mistake!" This is the perfect example of looking for love in all the wrong places. I was looking for the love that my father did not give me. Nobody and nothing can fill the void, only God. Most of my distractions came from seeking acceptance from men. All of these men were either toxic, broken, or insecure themselves. I didn't know what it was like to have a real, positive male in my life, so the counterfeits were accepted. I enjoyed their company until they wanted more from me. I even went as far as foreplay, but I didn't have sex with any of them because I didn't want to endure the pain I felt at the age of 7 years old. I was damaged mentally. As a matter of fact, my first marriage wasn't consummated and the second marriage was just a rebound. Say it again, "Big Mistake!"

I thank God that I am clothed in my right mind. After years of bumping my head, trying to do things my way, I finally stopped and wholeheartedly repented to God. I did a 360. Just like the GPS system, God reset my life. One thing about being on a detour, if you don't give up and continue on the path, you will eventually get to your destination. It may take a little longer than you had planned, but life lessons learned along the way will one day be worth the trip. This reminds me of the children of Israel, wandering around in the wilderness. It took them 40 years to complete an 11-day journey. Can you imagine setting out on a short trip and 40 years later is when you finally reach your destination? That was me. A whole generation was lost while they wandered in the wilderness. I cannot help but think about how much different my life would be if I would have taken a different path in life.

Romans 8:28 says, "And we know that all things work together for good to them that love God, to them who are the called according to his purpose."

No matter how you arrived at this point in your life, God can still get the glory.

The Message Bible states, "God himself willing and working at what will give Him the most pleasure" (Philippians 2:13).

One thing we need to learn is that God always has our best interest at heart. Just like the loving Father that He is, God is always looking out for us. He already knows what lies ahead of us. He knows that we will not always make the mark, but He loves us just the same.

Proverbs 3:5-6 says, "Trust in the Lord with all thine heart; and lean not unto thine own understanding. In all thy ways acknowledge Him and He shall direct thy paths."

I'm speaking to you from my own personal experience. I hope and pray that I am encouraging someone to put God first. Life is so much better with God at the wheel. God will forgive you and restore you. God did it for me and He surely can do the same for you.

2 Chronicles 7:14 says, "If my people, which are called by my name shall humble themselves and pray, and seek my face and turn from their wicked ways, then I will hear from heaven, will forgive their sins and heal their land."

As soon as you repent, God will forgive you. These detours that I put myself through all came about because I would not stop making my own choices. I did what I thought was best for me. These were distractions (aka needless pains) that I allowed. I could have saved myself from the many years of disappointments, pain, and hurt that I experienced while traveling down my own path. But God is so good. He allowed me to take that route so that I could see I didn't know what I thought I knew. Regardless of how old I was, I still needed to be like a child and let the Father lead me through life. It took many years to get this lesson, but I finally got it!

Taking an (L)esson
In life, lessons are taught.
In order to seek a dream, you gotta speak to the thought.
And sometimes you gotta practice silence in order to hear your faults.
Be willing to trade value to gain
Self-worth at all costs.
To find thyself, you have to take a loss to realize that you are lost.
But the L that you held is a Lesson, not a sign that you've failed so,
Prevail by living each day knowing that life is short.
Tomorrow may change its mind,
So be wise on how you decide to spend your time.
A crime it is not, to mess up or make mistakes.
That's another L, but oh well, that means you
Learned and have earned a blessing today.
Okay you ain't perfect, accept it,
No need to make that attempt,
You were made this way on purpose as a human,
And from error...no human's exempt.
In life, You gon' fall before you find your balance,
Stand up, dust it off and look forward to the next challenge.
Your crown is gonna be crooked,

Integrity will be compromised, but your faith will be restored.

And you'll learn how your smile can drown your cries.

You've died, 10 times inside, but your strength will resurrect.

Don't be afraid to pull up your sleeves and show the world your wounds

While you walk away with self-respect.

Self-doubt has had its final Bout,

You've knocked it out and it's down for the count.

A winner is born through all of the obstacles that he surmounts.

A mountain of despair will come tumbling in the midst of your highest climb,

But stay focused on your incline and once you've reached the top

You can rejoice in the feeling of being able to say,

"Victory is Mine!"

~S Hope

CHAPTER 7

Out of the Pan Into the Fire

THERE ARE MANY TRANSLATIONS to this fable "Out of the pan into the fire." One denotes that we are to avoid present dangers, lest we fall into worse perils." In other words, when a person goes from a bad situation into an even worse situation. This describes the next chapter of my life. I had waited six years for the possibility of a reconciliation with my husband. He kept asking me to wait for him to get himself together, but he was just stringing me along. I finally filed for divorce. The whole process lasted about a year. I started dating again before the divorce was finalized. Then I did the stupidest thing I could have done at this point. Six months after my divorce was finalized, I got married again. When I look back on that time in my life, all I can say is in Madea's voice, "What was I thinking?" That was the problem, I was not thinking. I did not give myself time to process and heal from the repercussions of what happened in my first marriage. Therefore, I was bringing baggage into yet another marriage that I knew deep down inside I should not have gotten into.

I was getting ready to turn 30 years old and the foolishness of thinking I was getting old as well as desperation came on me. This brings me to the title Out of the Pan and Into the Fire. From a bad situation into a worse situation. Again, I ignored the stop sign. The flags were waving but I ignored them. One thing you need to know is when you walk after the lusts of your flesh, it will override the spirit. Immediately after getting married, I knew I was up the creek without a paddle. I found myself in a situation, that oh my goodness, words cannot explain how I felt. I had given my virginity to my second husband so that bond (soul tie) had been formed, but I just knew it wasn't God ordained. He went to church, but he was not a spiritual man. He was religious without a relationship with God. It was another distraction.

I made more wrong decisions trying to fix my life, but instead I made things worse. Instead of getting it annulled and moving on with my life, I stayed and tried to make it work. Big Mistake! The longer I stayed, the worse it got. It was like trying to fit a square peg into a round hole. It was never going to work. This was not God ordained. "Can two walk together, except they be agreed" (Amos 3:3). But I figured it was my second marriage and I was going to do everything I could do to make it work (Again, doing things my own way.). Somebody say it again, "Big mistake!" Oh, what needless pain we bear, all because we do not carry everything to God in prayer.

So I was married again with two children (one disabled) and living a miserable life, going to church faithfully every week, every service. I remember crying on my way home from work because I didn't want to go home. I'm not saying that everything was his fault. I was not a whole woman. I was toxic, and in need of healing and deliverance myself. It is very difficult to be able to maintain a healthy relationship, especially if that person is toxic, insecure, and broken themselves. So this circus continued on and on for 20+ years. I allowed it to continue just to save face because I cared more about what other people had to say. Abuse is not only physical. It can be emotional, mental, verbal, financial or just negligence. Yes I was going to church week after week, serving in ministry. I even asked for a mediation meeting with my pastor and left out feeling ten times worse than when I went in. None of my issues were resolved. They made me feel like I was just nagging.

Here's the lesson I learned from this part of my life: No one can fix me but God. I tried to fix my marriage, but a half man is worse than having no man. I had to stop, evaluate my life and realize that I was the common denominator in this story and I had to fix myself. I was having daddy issues. I had no covering, teaching, protection, provision and spoken words of validation from my father, so I would latch onto any male who would show me any kind of attention. I had no self-worth and no self-esteem. I was still dealing with the sexual violation of my childhood. I admit I was a total mess and ok, at this point, I felt stuck.

CHAPTER 8

Stuck

I FELT STUCK. AT THIS point in my life, I had two children. We learned that our youngest child was having some health issues that would affect the rest of his life. He is physically disabled. "Ok, where are you going now?" The devil whispered in my ear. One time I called myself leaving, but I had no extra money saved, and no place to go with two children, so I went back home. I kept making excuses on why I should stay, but it was my low self-esteem and insecurity that held me hostage. Today I know if I would have left, God would have made a way of escape, but I did not have the faith and self-confidence to make the move. Year after year of embarrassment and neglect, manipulation, and control.

My twin sister, Doris, would always encourage me to see that I deserved better, but I couldn't see myself in that light. I was surrounded by so much negativity I could not see anything positive for myself. I became a puppet in another man's play. I allowed someone else to control my life. Yes, I was going to church faithfully, attending every single service. Besides my twin and one dear friend, Irene, no one said anything. Not even family members; they just watched and talked about me. This went on for years. One of my brothers said to me, "When you get tired enough, you will do something about it!" That statement helped push me to seek my own deliverance. That was the day that the lightbulb came on and I began to mentally plan my escape. I kept changing my mind. Therefore, it took years to finally walk away.

CHAPTER 9

My Wilderness Experience

I CO-AUTHORED A BOOK WITH Prophetess Kimberly Moses and 15 other authors titled, "It Cost Me Everything." I briefly wrote about how disobedience cost me almost everything. I said that disobedience is sin. It will cost you to forfeit the blessings and plans that God has for you. Partial and/or delayed obedience is still sin.

1 Samuel 15:22-23 says, "And Samuel said, 'Hath the Lord as great delight in burnt offerings and sacrifices, as in obeying the voice of the Lord? Behold, to obey is better than sacrifice, and to hearken than the fat of rams. For rebellion is as the sin of witchcraft and stubbornness is as iniquity and idolatry. Because thou hast rejected the word of the Lord he hath also rejected thee from being king.'"

I highly suggest that you read this book. It contains testimonies on several other topics and areas that the Body of Christ could benefit from. My wilderness experience began when I decided to leave my headquarters church to go to one of the affiliate churches. The new church was birthed out of a youth crusade ministry that I was a part of. I thought my Bishop would allow me to go along with the others, but he did not permit me to go. He recognized the anointing on my life. His job with the assistance of the Holy Spirit, was to groom me for my ministry assignment.

There were some areas in me that needed to be worked on in order for me to be able to carry the oil of the anointing on my life. I got impatient because I thought my bishop was punishing me. He gave others permission to leave to go to the new church, all except me. I had to stay at home. I was laughed at and talked about and it should have been ok with me, but the devil made me feel that I was being rejected again. But it was actually God trying to protect and groom me. He wanted to process me for my destiny.

At first, I obeyed even though I did not understand, but after a couple of years, I jumped off the Potter's wheel. The Potter's wheel is designed to fashion us into vessels of honor, fit for the Master's plan. God wanted to perfect that which concerneth me (Psalm 138:8) and to deliver me from me and all the stuff that was in me hindering me from maturing and blossoming into my intended purpose.

Romans 9:20-21 says, "Shall the thing formed say to him that formed it, why hast thou made me thus? Can the clay tell the potter how to form him? Hath not the potter power over the clay?" God is asking us in Jeremiah 18:6, "O house of Israel, cannot I do with you as this potter?" The potter (God) had a much bigger and better plan for my life.

Jeremiah 29:11 states, "For I know the thoughts that I think toward you," saith the Lord, "thoughts of peace, and not of evil, to give you an expected end."

1 Corinthians 2:9 states, "But as it is written, eye hath not seen, nor ear heard, neither have entered into the heart of man, the things which God hath prepared for them that love him."

As I've researched the history of the potter's wheel, I've learned that there are different stages in its production. It did not start out as a machine run by electricity to produce overnight. In the beginning, it took several days to produce one vessel. They used their hands and feet to cause the wheel to spin. Because of the increased demand for pots, several methods were developed to increase the coiling process. There is a demand for authentic vessels of honor capable of carrying the oil of the anointing to go through the whole process of purification. Because we refuse to stay on the potter's wheel until completion, there is a production of imitation vessels. Pots that are weak and leaky are unable to fulfill their purpose. Pots that collapse under pressure because they did not stay in the oven until the refiner's fire burned out/off the particles that would manifest when fiery trials came.

After leaving headquarters and going to the affiliate church, I was there a couple of years but felt uneasy about some things so I left. Instead of going back home to headquarters because of

My Wilderness Experience

pride and shame, I went to visit other churches. I found none compared to The Pentecostal House of Prayer of Deliverance, of Brooklyn, New York. They believe in holiness and deliverance. A year later, I received an offer from my cousin to come to Salisbury, Maryland to assist her with the birth of her new ministry. It sounded like a good idea to me at the time, so we moved from New York to Maryland in May 2004. The ministry was on fire. It started off power-packed, but shortly after that first year, the pastor lost focus of doing ministry. Secular things became more important than church services. I finally decided I had had enough and I stopped going to church.

Again, instead of going back home, I stayed in Maryland. I began to fellowship with churches there, but the pastors were controlling and manipulative using the pulpit to spread gossip and send messages to people in the congregation. In 2012, I was invited back home to participate in a Women's Day service. The Holy Spirit dealt with me concerning reconnecting back under the umbrella of The Pentecostal House of Prayer of Deliverance, Inc. Today my brand name is ReJoyce because God has given me another chance to get back on the potter's wheel and allow Him to make me over again another. "So he made it again another vessel, as seemed good to the potter to make it" (Jeremiah 18:4b).

I stopped the revolving door that led me to nowhere. I acknowledged my wrong, repented to God and wholeheartedly stopped trying to do life on my terms and my way. I started by asking God to "take my life and do something with it." I began to seek God by praying, fasting and daily reading His Word.

He began to transform my mind, thoughts and desires. God showed me myself and I did not like the person I saw. I knew there was someone greater inside of me and I wanted her to come forth and shine. I had to do the work to reset my life and allow God to do the rest.

CHAPTER 10

The End Of An Error/The End Of An Era

*E*VEN AS I AM writing this book and taking a walk down memory lane, the tears are flowing down my cheeks. I had made the biggest mistake of my life. I endured over 20 years of mental and emotional abuse from a man who had no clue what it meant to be the head of a family. He did what he thought was right in his own eyes. One day he told me how bad a mother and wife I was, all because I did not do what he told me to do. My opinions and thoughts were never considered. I was just supposed to follow his orders because as he recently said to me, "It's over your head!" He did whatever he wanted to do. I tolerated his bad decisions, indecisiveness, and immature behavior for over 20 years. He was and still is very toxic. So again today, I am reminded why I finally walked away. Even though we are divorced now, when he comes around to see our children, he still displays his toxic behavior. Since I am now more mature spiritually, I have begun doing spiritual warfare and pleading the Blood of Jesus and pronouncing peace in my house. I've learned to take authority in my house and accept nothing but peace.

I had to have that hard conversation with myself and be completely honest. I told Joyce, "This is not the life that God planned for you. I was raised by a single mom and through it all, I made it. Joyce, You can do this! You can make it because God is with you. I know God will provide what I need when I need it." Then I found Scriptures to confirm my declarations and I repeated them daily. I began to sing the old school songs that we sang for devotional service back in the day. It still took me several years to finally untie the chains that bound me because my mind was not totally made up. I changed my mind several times and tried to make the marriage work, but deep down inside, I was so miserable. I worried about my children, and what people would think, what people would say. Would I be able to continue in ministry?

For years I beat myself up. I knew I could make it on my own, but I fought with myself, making excuses. I wrestled with forgiving myself and self-condemnation. I realized that I'd made errors in my life, but I needed to close that door so that a new door/chapter could open. I wanted to reinvent the life that I felt God would have for me, but I had to put in the work to make it happen. I finally had enough of that foolishness and I filed for divorce. After over a year and a half of going back and forth to court and meetings, everything was finalized. I cannot explain to you that feeling of freedom. After being in bondage for so many years, I can now truthfully say I am enjoying my life. This is the very first time that I can say, "I enjoy being me."

CHAPTER 11

Repeat Defender

YOU CAN PLAY MIND games with yourself if you want, but the truth of the matter is that the devil will present to you exactly what he knows you like. Because you are saved does not mean that you do not have issues. Many of the saints that I've fellowshipped with throughout the last 40 years have issues. Most will not admit that they need some form of deliverance. They hide behind their titles, clothes and fake smiles. This is exactly what the devil wants them to do. As long as you stay in that state, you can never reach your full potential in the manifestations of God in your life. Thus flying with clipped wings. Well, that's exactly what happened to me.

There was a short period in time that I was very discouraged with my life. I found myself not desiring to go to the House of God. I slowly drifted away from my relationship with God. I spent most of my time at home and work. During this time, it was depressing as I was going through another divorce procedure for over a year. Divorce is very painful. Someone described the feeling of divorce as getting 1000 papercuts at the same time.

After some time, I met this guy. He claimed to be a Christian, but I found out that nowadays, everyone does. At first, he seemed to be a really nice guy. He seemed to have his life together. This was just another distraction to hinder me from pursuing my destiny. We talked occasionally, sharing life experiences. Of course, we talked about our children, work, and past relationships. The devil knows exactly how to reel you away from your purpose, and he will present that to you. Somehow Hezekiah Walker's song "Calling My Name" played in my spirit daily. It was God.

One afternoon he called and asked me to take a ride out with him to get a bite to eat. I agreed. This is one day that I will never forget. We called in our order in advance and when we arrived in the parking lot, we sat and began to talk. What happened next threw me for a loop. Out of the blue, he began by saying, "You better eat all your food and don't save none for your children." "OMG... huh, what? I've never done that!" I said. I was stunned as I sat there while he verbally went on a rampage for several minutes. He apologized but the damage was done. Then he gave me the money to go inside to pick up our food. This overwhelming feeling of helplessness came over me. By this time, I was scared and shocked, tears rolling down my face, I went straight to the bathroom to get myself together. I could not let anyone see me crying. He made me feel very low, like scum on the bottom of his shoes. How could someone say such mean things to me about my children? He had never met my children. At that moment, I knew I had to part ways from him. He turned out to be another counterfeit (distraction). To keep myself focused, I put a reminder on my cell phone that would ring every day at 4:44 p.m. that says, "I Deserve Better."

Oh No! I had done it again. I became a repeat defender. I almost fell for the foolishness once again by allowing a man to take the place in my life that he did not belong in. But not anymore. Another lesson learned. I turned my focus back on God and I began to spend a lot of time in prayer. One day as I sat quietly after my devotional time, I heard the Holy Spirit say, "Different face, same spirit." I was attracting the same kind of man because I was not a whole woman. I've made a conscious decision to change my life one day at a time, one step at a time. I prayed that God would change every area of my life. A few days after I prayed this prayer, Prophetess Juanita Bynum did a live posting on Facebook, confirming exactly what I prayed. I received it as confirmation that God let me know that He heard my prayer. He was transforming my thoughts and desires from pleasing my flesh to fulfilling His will for my life. I will not make excuses for the things that I've encountered in my life.

Some of them were self-inflicted wounds that I brought upon myself while others were beyond my control. Yet I refuse to live in the past. The past is the past. Everything that I've been through has taught me some valuable life lessons. Yet, I choose to be happy. Today, I can say I am better, stronger, and wiser. I am encouraged, strengthened and empowered to live a victorious life in God. I'm loving the Joyce that I am becoming. Her name is ReJoyce.

1 Peter 5:10-11 states, "But the God of all grace, who hath called us unto his eternal glory by Christ Jesus, after ye hath suffered a while, make you perfect, stablish, strengthen, settle you. To him be glory and dominion for ever and ever. Amen."

CHAPTER 12

The Road to Recovery

I'M WRITING THIS CHAPTER to help you understand that there is a process you must go through to get your deliverance and to be made whole. What I experienced is the result of not completing the healing process. The damage could have been avoided if I would've waited. Oh what needless pain we bear all because we do not carry everything to God in prayer. When we jump off of the Potter's wheel before the His approval, there will be situations to show you that you were not ready. The Potter (God) is the only One who knows when you are fully equipped and ready to move forward. We need to allow God to do the mending of all those unseen wounds, scars and bruises that we use make-up, red bottom shoes, fancy purses and fashionable clothes to hide. Underneath all of that are broken and wicked hearts. Please understand me. There is nothing wrong with those things; I like them myself, but what happens behind closed doors? How do you feel after the curtains are closed and the lights are turned off?

One important point I want to share with you is that there is no time limit for your healing to occur. The best home cooked meals take preparation and time to cook. There is no rush because the finished product will be worth the wait. I'm sharing my experience to hopefully encourage you to "wait on the Lord and be of good courage and He shall strengthen thy heart, wait I say on the Lord" (Psalm 27:14).

My experiences were in both ministry and relationships. I can wholeheartedly say that I thank God that my bishop made me wait. It was necessary. I am still on The Road to Recovery. Recovery is defined as a return to a normal state of health, mind, or strength. While in recovery, I cannot do all the things that I want to do. The process requires that sacrifices be made in order to heal properly. The devil wanted me to stay quiet because he is content with pushing things under the rug and acting like they never existed. The enemy also wanted me to stay in the state of self-condemnation. I felt stuck, not moving forward and not moving backwards. The road to recovery has not been easy, but it is possible. It takes a determined mindset and constant renewal of the mind through the Word of God.

Now to look back over the past 40 years, I have to admit I have not always walked the straight and narrow path of righteousness. "He that is without sin among you, let him first cast a stone at her (John 8:7)." Now I see this life from a different perspective. Besides coming totally clean with God and myself (I'm just being honest, that's the only way to be set free and delivered), I had to renounce all the negativity spoken over my life from my conception until now by family members, exes, friends and even some ministers. I had to take control over my life. When I came to the end of myself and admitted that I could not do life my own way, that's when God began to take over. My prayer was, "God, please take my life and do something with it." That's exactly what happened for me. After years of riding the merry-go-round, I finally surrendered my will over to God. Ever since that day, my life now is sweet and my walk with God has become a new adventure every day. I can truthfully say that I am enjoying my Christian walk. I'm working on becoming a better me, 'ReJoyce.'

SHE IS
She represents elegance, pride and grace,
defying impossibilities with her ability in every obstacle faced.
Her face never ruined by the tears that fall upon it,
her beauty only elevates as all fear and doubt are absconded.
She garnered wounds and scars from the weight of her mistakes,
but learned to carry her shoulders high as the moon and stars while confidence
levitates.
She never waits to be honored, instead she celebrates daily with a smile to smite
adversity,
Then walks tall after every stumble, never to fall, but standing stronger than
Hercules.
Sometimes it hurts to be the species of a soft and delicate expectancy,

but she revels in it, and wears her womanhood as a medal of fortitude respectively.

Her destiny lies in her challenges, and her pain and her triumph especially,

In every Woman there resides a Queen,

and I thank God, that I'm so blessed to be.

~S Hope

CHAPTER 13

Receipts

"You don't know the cost of the oil in my alabaster box." This is one of my favorite songs sung by CeCe Winans. When I think about this song, the word receipts comes to mind. This is my personal revelation of receipts. When you go to a store, the cashier hands you a receipt along with your change for the items you just purchased. A lot of times, I do not look at the receipt. I just tuck it away until I get home and then throw it into the garbage can. The receipt is a written statement of the proof of the purchase. If you need to return the item to the store, you will need a receipt. If the item is broken and/or damaged, you will need a receipt to prove that you actually bought the item from the store for the price marked. Without the receipt, you cannot prove your purchase.

Let's take a look at the receipts from a spiritual view. The record is in Heaven. Everything that I endured throughout my life has been stamped and approved. God allowed it. Just ask a veteran who served on the battlefield for this country. The experience that he/she has endured, no one can take it away. They will always and forever be a veteran. Another example is education. Once you learned that lesson, it can never be taken away from you. The oil in my alabaster box has been purchased through God's grace and mercy and the finished work on the cross through Jesus Christ. He paid the price for my deliverance, so my receipt is paid in full.

My identity was stolen during my childhood days, but I am now on the road to recovery. The sexual violation altered my path, but it did not steal my purpose. I'm not perfect, never was and never will be. This is my story, these are my truths, and this is my reality. I cannot change it. Dr. Yvonne Capehart said, "You cannot appreciate who you are today if you deny your yesterday." One thing I know for sure, no one can tell my story better than me. I have my receipts. God proved to be everything that He said He would be. I know God to be my Father, and so much more. I have my receipts. To God be the Glory. The devil tried to abort my purpose at a very young age, but God has reset my life. My receipt is stamped in red through the Blood of Jesus Christ PAID IN FULL!

CHAPTER 14

CLIPPED WINGS CAN STILL SOAR

WHAT SHALL WE THEN say to these things? If God be for us, who can be against us? (Romans 8:31 KJV) The Message Bible put it like this: "So, what do you think? With God on our side like this, how can we lose?" This is one of my favorite scriptures. According to the Word of God, there is nothing that can defeat us because God is with us, God is for us and God will fight for us. If it is in His will, you cannot be defeated!!

1 John 4:4 says, "Ye are of God, little children, and have overcome them: because greater is he that is in you, then he that is in the world."

If you are a believer in Jesus Christ and have accepted Him as your Lord and Savior, you will experience adversity. John 10:10 says, "The thief cometh not, but for to steal, and to kill, and to destroy; I am come that they might have life, and that they might have it more abundantly." Jesus is talking, giving us the three pointers on the purpose of our enemy. The devil comes to steal, to kill, and to destroy. He (the devil) is on his job 24/7. The devil fulfills his assignment, and he does it very well. He is consistent and purposeful in what he does. So why are we so surprised at what the devil does? If you are not facing any type of adversity in your life, you may want to check out your spiritual status and make sure you are still connected to the vine.

What does it mean to soar? According to the Merriam Webster dictionary, soar means to sail or hover in the air, often at a great height, to glide.

Despite what hand you have been dealt in life, it is your responsibility to play it out. Here is a quote from Bishop I.V. Hilliard, he said, "God gives each of us an even hand." I love to play the game of spades. When my family gets together, we always enjoy some good food, fun, laughter, jokes and most definitely several decks of cards for a game of spades. When the cards are dealt, you never know which card you will receive. Everyone would love to receive the Jokers and the Aces in every hand dealt, but you probably will not because there are multiple players. Your goal is to play the hand you are dealt with to the best of your ability to win the game. Sometimes we play with partners who will assist you to win the game. As it is in the game, we have a partner; He, The Holy Spirit, to assist us to win in this life.

The same scenario applies in life. We could not control which family we were born into. Neither could we control the color of our skin. The truth of the matter is, neither one of them are relevant to God. He loves us all the same. Some incidents that occur in our life beyond our control. There is a saying, "Life is 10 percent of what happens to you and 90 percent of how you respond to it." It is your responsibility for the outcome of your life. Joyce Meyer wrote, "Life sometimes gives you lemons, take them and make lemonade!" I need to repeat this. It is your responsibility on how your life turns out!

God has a plan and a purpose for your life. (Jeremiah 29:11, KJV, "For I know the thoughts that I think towards you, saith the Lord, thoughts of peace, and not of evil, to give you an expected end.) It is our responsibility to find out what our purpose is and walk in it. The choice is yours. Now you can take the lemons and add some sugar to make lemonade, take a sip and keep it moving or you can sit and mope and complain and blame others for your pity party until you die. The decision I made is to fly because:

"CLIPPED WINGS CAN STILL SOAR"

Most of the people I know personally who are highly anointed by God have faced some sort of adversity in their youth, most before the age of 10. This is because the enemy of our soul tried early in our lives to prevent us from fulfilling our purpose. The final decision was up to me. It was my call and my decision. Unfortunately, I made the wrong choices. I allowed my adversaries to dictate how my life would be. I sat on the sideline and just let life pass me by for many years. I did not try to change anything. I did not make the necessary adjustments. For many years, I allowed others to predict the outcome of my life. I aimlessly strolled through life, knowing on the inside of me that I had a greater purpose. I was too weak to fight. Spiritual warfare was in full force all the time and I refused to fight. I had received several Words of prophecy on what God's plans were for my life, but I could not rise above it. Adversity can make you stay stuck or motivate you to push forward. I felt like a deflated balloon where all the air had been knocked out of me. I was still functioning as a wife, mother, full-time employee, and had missionary duties at church, but spiritually it felt like I was just beating the air. I made little impact on the Kingdom of darkness. The strongholds held me captive and no one came to my rescue. I was on a merry go round, waiting for it to stop. (Sidebar: This is the reason why it is so vitally important to be careful who you connect with, some are just leeches that come to suck the life out of you)

Listed below are some of the reasons for my "Clipped Wings."

#1 When I was a little girl, I wanted to be a teacher. My mother said "NO."

#2 When I was a little girl, I also wanted to become a beautician. My mother said "NO."

#3 When I was a little girl, I wanted to run track. My mother said "NO" because I had asthma.

#4 When I was a teenager, I wanted to learn how to play the organ. When I shared it with one of the Pastors of the

Church, he laughed and called me piano fingers. I did not take it as a compliment. Instead, I felt embarrassed and ashamed of my long skinny fingers. Lastly, I even tried to get one of my brothers in Christ to show me how to keep a beat for devotional service. After one maybe two tries, he did not want to be bothered anymore. He recently joked about it saying, "I was a hot mess."

#5 I wanted to learn how to sing. My voice was always cracking somewhere between alto and tenor. I was embarrassed a lot in choir rehearsal, so I learned how to lip sing instead.

#6 A few years ago, I mentioned to someone my desire to open a shelter for women trying to get out of abusive relationships and do not have any money or place to go with their children. This person shot my dream idea out of the sky. She started out with Why? Then Blah, Blah, Blah, and I was like, oh never mind!

The six examples that I previously mentioned are some of the reasons that clipped my wings. I ALLOWED other people to "clip my wings" and I ALLOWED other people to tell me what I could and could not do. I valued other people's opinions over what God was telling me to do. They are dream killers. It is a negative toxic poison that the devil uses to attempt to destroy your potential. Experience and life have taught me not to share my visions and dreams prematurely because most of the time, instead of receiving encouragement, you get criticism. Now I walk in silence.

In the 1990's, I was the Vice-President of the Worldwide Youth Crusade of Deliverance. We traveled to many churches from New York to Georgia with deliverance services. One Saturday morning, we had a fundraiser breakfast to help raise money for our trips. I remember the preacher, the late Pastor Delric Pollins preached "Overcoming Public Opinion." It was a power-packed life-changing sermon just for me. I recorded the sermon and repeatedly played it to strengthen and encourage myself.

FLYING WITH CLIPPED WINGS.

As Christians (Christ-followers and disciples), we have the Holy Spirit who will walk alongside us to make sure that we win in our spiritual walk. We must be obedient to Him. Isaiah 1:19 states, "If ye be willing and obedient, ye shall eat the good of the land." Here is where my problem was; I was disobedient, and it caused me to miss out on many opportunities. I thank God for His love, mercy, and grace.

Let me take a moment to encourage you today. No matter what bad decisions you have made in your past, our God can restore you into good standing with Him and bless your life abundantly. Once you have acknowledged your wrongdoings, repent and turn from it, and God will miraculously change your life. I am a witness that God loves us so much and He always desires the best for us.

Isaiah 43:19 states, "Behold, I will do a new thing; now it shall spring forth; shall ye not know it? I will even make a way in the wilderness, and rivers in the desert."

Bishop Jakes said, "Use your wings and fly."
STILL, I RISE...
I shall be what God called me to be! Speaking the Word of God with daily confessions will change your whole world. Yes, adversity came, and it (temporarily) slowed me down, but today I am declaring that I am more than a conqueror! I do not blame anyone else but myself. After I repented before the Father, He picked me up, turned me around, and placed my feet on a plain path. I am moving forward, forgetting those things behind me, and I am reaching forth unto those things before. I press toward the mark for the prize of the high calling of God in Christ Jesus (Philippians 3:13-14).

Still, I Rise!! God has revived and rejuvenated my life. I am restored and resurrected to live the life that God purposed me to be. ReJoyce...She has awakened! She has vision, and a passion to pursue her dreams and to fulfill her destiny. Can these bones live? YES, and I shall not die, but live, and declare the works of the Lord (Psalm 118:17). Those hast turned for me my mourning into dancing: thou hast put off my sackcloth, and girded me with gladness (Psalm 30:11).

Still, I Rise!! I arise out of the ashes!! I am going to strengthen that which remains and work it!!

Out of the ashes we, the Holy Spirit, and I have birthed out: (1) The Touch of Hope Christian Counseling Services (www.touch4hope.org)(2) an Intercessory prayer call every Monday and Thursday morning @ 5:30am EST@ 609-663-1405) (2) I'm Just Saying E-book series (3) Strength for the Journey ministry of encouragement for Caregivers on Facebook and Instagram as well as an E-book and last but not least we have birthed out ReJoyce Enterprises, LLC. (rejoyce.prizes@gmail.com)

TO GOD BE THE GLORY!

I'M FLYING WITH CLIPPED WINGS

BECAUSE CLIPPED WINGS CAN STILL SOAR!!

CHAPTER 15

My Truths-My Realities-My Story

MY BEGINNING WAS VERY humble. I grew up poor in a single-parent home. That was my normal. WHAT IS NORMAL to you may be dysfunctional to others. But to God be the Glory! I asked God, "WHY NEW YORK CITY"? and the answer I received was "For I know the thoughts that I think toward you," saith the Lord, "thoughts of peace, and not of evil, to give you an expected end" (Jeremiah 29:11). I wore a RED JACKET because I was a LEAKING FAUCET. I had allowed the DETOURS AND DISTRACTIONS that the enemy sent to make me jump OUT OF THE PAN INTO THE FIRE. Then I found myself STUCK in MY WILDERNESS EXPERIENCE that felt like a whirlwind. I had to look myself in the mirror and forgive myself for trying to do things my own way. This was the beginning of my new season and THE END OF AN ERA, THE END OF AN ERROR. But I didn't fully learn my lesson. I became a REPEAT DEFENDER one last time. But after that last experience, I finally learned my lesson and now I'm on THE ROAD TO RECOVERY. Whether you believe me or not, I have THE RECEIPTS for all the pain, hurt, disappointments and rejections that I've endured throughout my life from family and friends. It's okay now because the devil tried to clip my wings and purpose for living, but he is a liar and a defeated foe and I'm facing my truths and my reality. I pray that one day God will use my transparency and my tests and turn them into a testimony for His Glory. I pray that you have enjoyed this book. I ask that you pray for me as I walk out my purpose.

I appreciate you for taking the time to read my book. Thank you and God bless you.
~**~

I'm happy from the inside out and from the outside in,
I'm firmly formed,
You canceled my ticket to hell – that's not my destination!
Now you've got my feet on the life path
All radiant from the shining of your face
Ever since you took my hand
I'm on the right way.
Psalm 16:9-11, The Message (MSG)
To God Be The Glory !

About The Author

Joyce was born 2nd of an unexpected set of twins in Accomac County, Virginia. At the age of four, her mother relocated to the Bedford Stuyvesant section of Brooklyn, New York.

At the tender age of 14 years old, Joyce accepted Jesus Christ as her personal Savior. She became a member of the Mt. Zion Pentecostal Holiness Church, where she received her Christian foundation and Biblical teaching.

In 1988, Joyce joined the Pentecostal House of Prayer of Deliverance Inc. under the tutelage of Chief Prelate Bishop McKinley Green, in Brooklyn, New York. Joyce was ordained as an Elder in October 2014.

Joyce attended Bethel Bible Institute from Fall 1991 to Spring 1997. She is currently pursuing a degree in Theology from the Dominion Theological Seminary.

Joyce is the mother of two, Shekinah and Philip, and a mentor to many.

She also has an identical twin sister who shares her love and passion for prayer and writing.

Joyce co-authored two books and has recently started an E-books series titled "I'm Just Saying" @ https://payhip.com/b/A7zp with many more on the way. She is the founder of A Touch of Hope Christian Counselling Services (www.touch-4hope.org). Joyce is also the founder of ReJoyce Enterprises, LLC. (rejoyce.prizes@gmail.com) You may contact Joyce on social media, Facebook @ Joyce Hope, Instagram @ Joyce.hope.5203, or email at www.joycehope.net or www.rejoyce7.com, Paypal.me/ReJoyce7 or cash app $ReJoyce7

Index

1

1960s, 7

A

ability, 3, 51, 56
abundantly, 55, 60
abuse, 24, 43
Abuse, 35
abuser, 24
acceptance, 28
accepted, 14, 25, 28, 55, 65
Accomack, 4, 6, 12, 13, 15
Accomack County, 4, 13
Aces, 56
acknowledge, 23, 30
adjustments, 57
adult world, 21
adversaries, 57

adversity, 51, 55, 56, 57, 61
affection, 22
affirmation, 24
afraid, 32
air, 3, 17, 56, 58
alabaster box, 53, 54
alcoholic, 10, 13
altar call, 4
alto, 59
anemia, 4
anger, 23
angry, 24
anointed, 21, 57
anointing, 39, 40
apologized, 22, 46
Apostle John Eckhardt, 8
appreciate, 10, 54, 64
appreciation, 3, 4, 23
approval, 49
approved, 53
argue, 24
argued, 9
article, 3
ashamed, 2, 20, 59
ashes, 61, 62
assignment, 39, 56
asthma, 4, 17, 58
Aunt Betty, 7, 17
aunts, 7
authority, 44

Index

authors, 38, 65
awakened, 61

B

B, 9
baby, 4
babysitter, 7
bad, 1, 16, 27, 33, 34, 43, 60
baggage, 33
Baptist church, 14
beautician, 58
beauty, 51
beginning, 6, 15, 40, 63
behavior, 3, 23, 43
Bethel Bible Institute, 65
bible study, 14
bicycle, 16
bike, 16
bills, 10, 28
Birds, 3
birthday, 3, 4
birthed, 39, 62
Bishop, 18, 39, 56, 61, 65
Bishop George Bloomer, 18
bitter, 24
bitterness, 23
blame, 57, 61
bleeding, 24
blessed, 52

blessing, 31
blessings, 2, 38
blossoming, 39
bondage, 2, 22, 44
book, 1, 2, 10, 38, 43, 62, 64, 65
boot camp, 13
born, 4, 6, 13, 15, 32, 56, 65
bound, 22, 44
brain aneurysm, 19
breakthrough, 22
breeding, 4
Broadway, 10
broken, 3, 23, 28, 35, 49, 53
Brooklyn, 7, 15, 41, 65
brother, 6, 10
bruises, 49
budget, 18
burden, 23
busy, 14, 15

C

cantankerous, 24
captive, 58
car, 16, 20
Caregivers, 62
Cash app, 64
cashier, 53
CeCe Winans, 53
cell phone, 47

Index

chains, 2, 44
challenge, 31
chapter, 18, 33, 44, 45, 49
character, 2
cheerful, 20
child, 4, 9, 21, 31, 36
childhood, 4, 7, 17, 20, 22, 35, 54
children, 6, 10, 12, 23, 24, 29, 34, 36, 43, 44, 46, 55, 59, 65
choices, 1, 30, 57
choir rehearsal, 59
Christ, 14, 22, 24, 38, 48, 54, 55, 59, 60, 61, 65
Christian, 15, 46, 51, 62, 65
church, 4, 14, 17, 18, 27, 28, 34, 35, 36, 38, 39, 40, 41, 58
churches, 39, 41, 60
circus, 35
clay, 39
clean, 5, 50
clipped wings, 3, 4, 45
Clipped Wings, 2, 3, 5, 6, 58, 60
closet, 20
clothes, 10, 20, 45, 49
clothing, 5
Collins English Dictionary, 24
comfort zone, 12
complain, 10, 24, 57
completion, 40
compliments, 22
compromised, 32
conception, 50
condemnation, 2, 19, 21, 44, 50

confessions, 25, 61
confidence, 51
confirmation, 3, 47
congregation, 41
conqueror, 61
consummated, 29
control, 2, 36, 47, 51, 56, 57
controversy, 3
conversation, 18, 44
counseling session, 17
counterfeits, 28
cousins, 7
covering, 35
co-workers, 3
crime, 31
criticism, 59
crooked, 31
cross, 16, 54
crown, 31
crying, 34, 46
curses, 23
curtains, 49

D

daddy, 9, 13, 23, 35
damage, 22, 23, 24, 46, 49
damaged soul, 24
dancing, 61
danger, 4

darkness, 58
Daryl, 7
daughter, 14, 23, 24
daughters, 6, 7
death, 6, 13
decision, 47, 57
decisions, 1, 26, 34, 43, 60
declarations, 44
defame, 2
defeated, 55, 64
defender, 47
degrees, 19
deliver, 2, 39
deliverance, 2, 4, 18, 21, 22, 25, 35, 37, 41, 45, 49, 54, 60
Delric Pollins, 60
denial, 24
denominator, 35
depressed, 28
depressing, 45
desert, 61
despair, 32
desperation, 34
despise, 23
destination, 26, 29, 64
destiny, 8, 13, 26, 39, 46, 52, 61
destroy, 55, 56, 59
details, 2, 17
detours, 26, 30
Deuteronomy, 15
devalue, 3

devil, 22, 27, 36, 39, 45, 46, 50, 54, 55, 56, 59, 64

devotional, 44, 47, 59

dictate, 1, 57

die, 57, 61

died, 6, 32

dinner table, 7

disappointments, 30, 64

discern, 21

discerned, 18

discouraged, 45

disobedience, 38

distracted, 27

divine plan, 26

divorce, 33, 44, 45

divorced, 18, 43

doctor, 6

dodgeball, 7

dominion, 48

Dominion Global Bible Institute and Seminary, 65

Doris, 36

doubt, 51

doubted, 21

Dr. Becker, 3

Dr. Tony Evans, 26

Dr. Yvonne Capehart, 54

dream, 9, 31, 59

dreams, 59, 61

driver, 16

Dwayne, 7

dysfunction, 9, 10

Index

dysfunctional, 63

E

ear, 22, 36, 40
Eastern Shore, 13
education, 53
effectual fervent prayer, 18
electricity, 40
elegance, 51
embarrassed, 28, 59
embarrassment, 19, 21, 36
emotional, 35, 43
empowered, 47
encourage, 36, 50, 60
encouraged, 4, 7, 18, 23, 47
encouragement, 2, 22, 24, 59, 62
encouraging, 30
endured, 1, 4, 43, 53, 64
enemy, 8, 50, 55, 57, 63
environment, 13, 15
ERA, 63
error, 31
ERROR, 63
escape, 4, 36, 37
eternal, 48
excuses, 22, 36, 44, 47
expectancy, 51
eye, 40

F

Facebook, 18, 47, 62, 64, 65
faith, 7, 32, 36
false sense, 20
family, 9, 13, 14, 19, 36, 43, 50, 56, 64
fancy purses, 49
fantasize, 12
fasting, 41
father, 9, 10, 28, 35
Father, 10, 11, 30, 31, 54, 61
fatherless, 8
Fatherlessness, 8
fault, 24, 25, 35
faults, 18, 31
fear, 17, 51
fellowship, 41
financial support, 10
fire, 33, 40, 41
FIRE, 63
flags, 34
flight, 3
fly, 3, 57, 61
Flying, 2, 3, 5, 60
focus, 21, 27, 41, 47
food, 4, 10, 46, 56
food stamps, 4, 10
foolishness, 34, 44, 47
foreplay, 29
forgive, 22, 30, 63

forgiveness, 25
fortitude, 52
fought, 9, 10, 44
foundation, 14, 15, 65
free, 2, 22, 50
freedom, 25, 44
friends, 3, 13, 14, 19, 28, 51, 64
frustrations, 23
fun, 24, 56
fundraiser, 60
fussed, 9, 23
future, 1, 8

G

games, 7, 45
garments, 15
generation, 23, 29
generational, 23
generations, 15
girlfriend, 17
gladness, 61
glory, 1, 29, 48
Glory, 4, 13, 54, 63, 64
God, 1, 2, 3, 4, 5, 6, 7, 9, 10, 11, 12, 13, 14, 15, 17, 18, 19, 21, 22, 25, 26, 27, 28, 29, 30, 31, 34, 35, 36, 38, 39, 40, 41, 42, 44, 45, 46, 47, 48, 49, 50, 51, 52, 53, 54, 55, 56, 57, 58, 59, 60, 61, 63, 64
good, 1, 13, 15, 22, 23, 24, 28, 29, 31, 41, 50, 56, 60
goodness, 34
gossip, 18, 41

government cheese, 10
GPS, 26, 29
grace, 48, 51, 54, 60
graduation, 17, 28
grandparents, 12
greeted, 19
Grinch, 24
guilt, 19, 21

H

hair, 28
hallway, 7
Halsey Street, 7
Hancock Street, 7
happy, 11, 20, 47, 64
headquarters, 38, 40
heal, 2, 22, 30, 33, 50
healed, 17, 18
healing, 2, 24, 25, 35, 49, 50
health issues, 36
healthy, 35
heart, 22, 30, 40, 50
heartbroken, 22
heaven, 30
helplessness, 46
hesitant, 4
Hezekiah Walker, 46
hide-and-go-seek, 7
high calling, 61

high school, 15, 17, 27, 28
hindering, 39
history, 40
holiness, 41
holy, 14
Holy Spirit, 3, 4, 14, 22, 24, 39, 41, 47, 56, 60, 62
honest, 27, 44, 50
honored, 51
hope, 2, 30
hopscotch, 7
hospital, 16, 17
hospitals, 14
hostage, 36
house, 6, 7, 17, 28, 39, 44
household, 9, 10
hugs, 22
humble, 11, 30, 63
hurt, 2, 6, 10, 16, 21, 22, 24, 30
hurtful, 22
hurting, 22, 24
husband, 33, 34

I

I love you, 22
identity, 54
idolatry, 38
imagine, 12, 13, 29
imitation vessels, 40
immature, 43

impatient, 39
impossibilities, 51
inconsistency, 28
increase, 6, 40
indecisiveness, 43
infectious disease, 6
iniquity, 38
insecure, 28, 35
insecurities, 3
insecurity, 36
Instagram, 62
instinct, 3
Integrity, 32
interest, 30
Irene, 36
issue, 3
It Cost Me Everything, 38

J

jacks, 7
James, 6, 18
Jesus, 2, 13, 14, 22, 23, 43, 48, 54, 55, 61, 65
job, 3, 12, 28, 39, 56
Jokers, 56
jokes, 10, 56
journey, 1, 4, 15, 29
joy, 13
Joyce, 44, 47, 57, 64, 65
judging, 18

jump rope, 7

K

kid, 10
kill, 55, 56
killjoy, 24
Kimberly, 38
King, 13
King Herod, 13

L

Lamb, 2
laughed, 19, 39
laughter, 56
leaky faucet, 24
leftovers, 4
legalism, 15
lemonade, 57
lemons, 57
lessons, 13, 29, 31, 47
liberty, 22
library, 28
life, 1, 2, 4, 6, 7, 9, 12, 13, 14, 20, 21, 24, 25, 26, 27, 28, 29, 31, 33, 34, 35, 36, 39, 40, 41, 42, 43, 44, 45, 46, 47, 50, 51, 53, 54, 55, 56, 57, 58, 59, 60, 61, 64, 65
light, 16, 36
lightbulb, 37
lips, 23

lives, 2, 22, 57
loss, 6, 31
love, 22, 28, 29, 40, 56, 60, 65
loved, 9, 18, 22, 23, 24
loves, 30, 57, 60
low self-esteem, 21, 36
lustful, 17

M

macaroni and cheese, 10
Madea, 33
male, 28, 35
manifestations, 45
manipulation, 36
marriage, 17, 29, 33, 34, 35, 44
married, 17, 27, 28, 33, 34
marry, 12, 28
Maryland, 41
Master's plan, 2, 39
mating, 4
matured, 11
McKinley Green, 65
mediation, 35
memories, 7, 13, 16
memory lane, 43
mental, 17, 35, 43
mercy, 1, 54, 60
Merriam Webster dictionary, 24, 56
merry-go-round, 27, 51

Message Bible, 30, 55
Meyer, 57
mighty, 2, 13
mind, 3, 10, 22, 29, 31, 37, 42, 44, 45, 50, 53, 59
minister, 3, 4, 27
ministers, 14, 51
ministry, 4, 35, 39, 41, 44, 50, 62
miraculously, 60
miserable, 34, 44
Miss Hall, 7
Mistake, 28, 29, 34
mistakes, 1, 2, 27, 31, 51
money, 10, 36, 46, 59, 60
Moses, 12, 13, 38
mother, 4, 6, 7, 9, 10, 13, 14, 16, 22, 23, 24, 28, 43, 58, 65
Mother Hattie Green, 3
mourning, 61

N

nagging, 35
naïve, 27
name brand sneakers, 5
needed, 4, 10, 22, 25, 31, 39, 44
needless pains, 30
negative, 15, 23, 24, 25, 59
negative influence, 15
negative words, 23, 25
neglect, 24, 36
negligence, 35

neighborhood, 7, 14
nesting sites, 4
New York, 6, 7, 12, 13, 15, 16, 41, 60, 65
New York City, 7, 12, 13
normal, 9, 10, 11, 50, 63
nursing homes, 14

O

Oak Cliff Bible Fellowship, 26
obedient, 22, 60
obey, 21, 38
obstacle, 51
offerings, 38
oil, 39, 40, 53, 54
opinions, 43, 59
opportunities, 4, 60
organ, 58
Orphan, 8
outcome, 57
overcame, 2
overjoyed, 4
owner, 3, 16

P

pain, 6, 17, 19, 23, 24, 29, 30, 34, 49, 52, 63
pan, 33
pants, 15
paralysis, 6

Index

parents, 9, 12
park, 19
parties, 4
party pooper, 24
passion, 61, 65
past, 1, 2, 24, 25, 46, 47, 50, 60
Pastor, 1, 18, 26, 60
pastors, 14, 17, 41
path, 15, 29, 31, 50, 54, 61, 64
paths, 13, 30
patients, 14
peace, 40, 43, 44, 57, 63
peanut butter, 10
Pentecostal Holiness Church, 14, 23, 65
Pentecostal House of Prayer of Deliverance, 41, 65
perfect, 28, 31, 39, 48, 54
perils, 33
perverted spirit, 17
Pharaoh, 12
Philistines, 12
piano fingers, 59
pick up sticks, 7
pity party, 57
pleasure, 3, 30
polio, 6
poor, 11, 63
positive role model, 24
potential, 3, 45, 59
potter, 39, 40, 41
Potter's wheel, 39, 49

poverty, 6
power, 39, 41, 60
powerful, 21
pray, 2, 14, 18, 21, 30, 64
prayer, 14, 34, 47, 49, 51, 62, 65
praying, 4, 41
predation, 4
Prevail, 31
pride, 41, 51
privilege, 9
problem, 24, 33, 60
process, 2, 25, 33, 39, 40, 49, 50
promiscuous, 17
prophecy, 58
Prophetess Juanita Bynum, 47
Prophetess Tina, 21
protect, 9, 39
protected, 15, 19
protection, 20, 35
provision, 35
pulpit, 41
purchase, 16, 53
purification, 40
purpose, 2, 3, 8, 26, 29, 31, 39, 40, 46, 54, 55, 57, 58, 64
pursue, 61

Q

Queen, 52

R

radiant, 64
rams, 38
real, 1, 7, 13, 28
reality, 1, 18, 19, 21, 24, 54, 64
rebound, 29
receipt, 53, 54
receipts, 53, 54
reconciliation, 33
red bottom shoes, 49
red jacket, 18, 19, 20
refused, 21, 58
regret, 10, 15, 24
rejected, 22, 23, 38, 39
rejection, 23
rejoice, 32
ReJoyce, 41, 47, 51, 61, 62
relationships, 3, 46, 50, 59
relatives, 3
relevant, 1, 57
religious, 34
renounce, 23, 25, 50
repair, 23
repent, 30, 60
repented, 25, 29, 41, 61
repercussions, 33
rescue, 58
responsibility, 25, 56, 57
restore, 30, 60

restored, 32, 61
resurrect, 32
resurrected, 61
reunion, 18, 19
revival, 4, 14
revolving door, 12, 27, 41
righteous man, 18
rivers, 61
Road to Recovery, 49, 50
roadmap, 26
rollercoaster, 2
route, 26, 31
rules, 15

S

sackcloth, 61
sacrifices, 38, 50
sadness, 13
saints, 18, 21, 22, 45
salvation, 2
save, 2, 35, 46
saved, 1, 12, 13, 14, 15, 17, 18, 30, 36, 45
Savior, 14, 55, 65
scar, 2
scars, 49, 51
Scripture, 8, 15
secret, 19
security blanket, 19
self-confidence, 36

Self-doubt, 32
self-esteem, 35
self-respect, 32
self-worth, 21, 35
sermon, 60
served, 4, 9, 12, 53
service, 3, 4, 14, 23, 28, 34, 36, 41, 44, 59
sex, 17, 29
sexual advancements, 17
sexual desires, 17, 21
sexual violation, 35, 54
sexually violated, 17, 21
shame, 19, 21, 41
shelter, 59
Shepherd, 3, 4
silence, 31, 59
sin, 15, 38, 50
single parent, 4, 13, 23
single-parent, 9, 63
sins, 14, 18, 30
sister, 6, 18
situations, 1, 2, 22, 49
skelly, 7
skin, 13, 56
smile, 32, 51
smiles, 45
social media, 64, 65
socialize, 4
soul, 34, 57
spades, 56

spinal cord, 6
Spirit, 3, 7, 8, 14, 22
spirit of rejection, 23
spiritual battle, 18
spiritual encounter, 14
spiritual man, 34
spiritual walk, 27, 60
spiritual warfare, 43
stamped, 53, 54
steal, 54, 55, 56
steps, 15
Steven Furtick, 1
store, 10, 19, 53
story, 1, 2, 18, 21, 35, 54
street, 14, 16
strength, 8, 32, 50
strengthen, 48, 50, 60, 61
strong, 2
stronger, 2, 47, 51
strongholds, 58
stubbornness, 38
stuck, 35, 36, 50, 58
stumble, 51
suffered, 48
sugar, 57
suicide, 22
Sunday school, 14
surrendered, 4, 51
swim, 16
swimming pool, 16

T

tag, 7
Tammy Moore, 18
tangible presence, 14
teacher, 58
teaching,, 35
tears, 4, 13, 43, 46, 51
tenor, 59
testimonies, 38
testimony, 2, 64
tests, 64
thank, 29, 50, 52, 60
thoughts, 40, 42, 43, 47, 57, 63
ticket, 64
tired, 37
titles, 45
Tompkins Avenue, 7
toxic, 23, 28, 35, 43, 59
transforming, 47
transparency, 1, 64
traumatic, 17, 22
traveled, 12, 60
trials, 4, 40
triumph, 52
true, 24
truth, 18, 21, 25, 27, 45, 56
truths, 1, 2, 18, 54, 64
TV, 27

twin sister, 6, 7, 16, 17, 36, 65
two-parent home, 9

U

ugly, 1
unclean spirits, 18
understanding, 26, 30
unpleasant, 24
unresolved issues, 24
unwilling, 24
usher, 28

V

vaccine, 6
validation, 35
valuable, 47
value, 31
vessel, 40, 41
vessels of honor, 39, 40
veteran, 53
vibrant, 20
Vice-President, 60
victorious, 47
vine, 56
Virginia, 4, 6, 7, 12, 13, 15, 65
vision, 8, 61
voice, 23, 26, 33, 38, 59
void, 28

Index

W

warning signs, 27
water, 16, 17
water park, 16
weak, 40, 58
wedding, 28
weight, 28, 51
well-groomed, 5
whispered, 22, 36
wholeheartedly, 18, 29, 41, 50
wicked, 30, 49
wilderness, 29, 38, 61
willing, 30, 31, 60
wings, 3, 4, 21, 59, 61, 64
wise, 31
witchcraft, 38
woman, 1, 2, 13, 21, 35, 47
womanhood, 52
Women's Day, 41
Word of God, 2, 4, 27, 50, 55, 61
word of knowledge, 21
world, 1, 32, 55, 61
Worldwide Youth Crusade of Deliverance, 60
wounds, 32, 47, 49, 51

Y

youngest, 6, 36

FLYING WITH CLIPPED WINGS

www.ingramcontent.com/pod-product-compliance
Lightning Source LLC
Chambersburg PA
CBHW050329120526
44592CB00014B/2115